Blogging For Profit

The No-Nonsense Beginner's

Blueprint To Earn Money Online

With Your Blog

▲▼▲▼▲▼▲▼▲▼▲▼▲▼▲▼▲▼▲▼▲▼▲▼▲▼▲▼

Phil C. Senior

Bluesource And Friends

This book is brought to you by Bluesource And Friends, a happy book publishing company.

Our motto is **"Happiness Within Pages"**
We promise to deliver amazing value to readers with our books.
We also appreciate honest book reviews from our readers.

Connect with us on our Facebook page www.facebook.com/bluesourceandfriends and stay tuned to our latest book promotions and free giveaways.

Don't forget to claim your FREE books!

Brain Teasers:

https://tinyurl.com/karenbrainteasers

Harry Potter Trivia:

https://tinyurl.com/wizardworldtrivia

Sherlock Puzzle Book (Volume 2)

https://tinyurl.com/Sherlockpuzzlebook2

Also check out our best seller book

"67 Lateral Thinking Puzzles"

https://tinyurl.com/thinkingandriddles

Table of Contents

Bluesource And Friends

Introduction

Chapter 1:

What are you going to blog about?

But shouldn't it be as broad as possible so I can reach more people?

Well, first you're going to just pick something

And choose one

Now that you have a general idea, it's time to do some market research

Determining if your niche is profitable

Who will you be talking to?

How to create your perfect Ideal Customer Avatar

Chapter 2:

Choosing your blog's name and domain

Finding a host for your blog

What should you look for in a good blog host?

Some services to consider:

Deciding on a blogging platform

What should you look for in a good CMS?

Some services to consider

Choosing a theme and designing your blog

What should you look for in a good theme?

Chapter 3:

To begin, stop and think

Writing product descriptions that sell

A few tips:

Selling other people's products and services

Chapter 4:

How to make a weekly publishing schedule a little less time-consuming

How to batch your work

How to write a blog post

Organizing your content

Here's a couple of tips:

Chapter 5:

Here are a few ways to narrow it down:

Next steps

Chapter 6:

Email Lists

What makes email lists so important to your business?

How to build an email list

One last note

Chapter 7:

Here are some tips and tricks for making money with your email list:

Chapter 8:

How much money can a blogger make

How to make money as a blogger

Prepare to have multiple streams of income

Prepare to constantly produce valuable, free content

Find one or two bloggers to model and learn from, but DON'T try to copy them!

Chapter 9:

Hosting

Email service providers

Learning about blogging/marketing

Blogging For Profit

Monetization

Landing Pages

SEO

Productivity

Design/Branding

Analytics

Marketing/Social Media

Writing

Conclusion

Introduction

▲▼▲▼▲▼▲▼▲▼▲▼▲▼▲▼▲▼▲▼▲▼▲▼▲▼▲▼▲▼

Congratulations on getting *Blogging for Profit: The No-Nonsense Beginner's Blueprint To Earn Money Online With Your Blog* and thank you for doing so.

The following chapters will discuss everything you need to know to build and grow a profitable blog. We'll talk about choosing a subject and an audience, designing a professional and trust-building website, deciding what products and services you'll provide, showing up for your audience every week, utilizing social media to generate traffic to your site, selling to your own personal fan base, and making money with your blog through alternative means.

Throughout this book, I have tried to provide an easy-to-follow process for building and growing your blog. You can absolutely read through the entire book before taking action, but I designed this book to serve as a guide to walk you through the process. Use this book however you learn best!

There are plenty of books on this subject on the market, so thanks again for choosing this one! Every effort was made to ensure it is full of as much useful information as possible. Please enjoy!

Chapter 1:

▲▼▲▼▲▼▲▼▲▼▲▼▲▼▲▼▲▼▲▼▲▼▲▼▲▼▲▼▲▼

Now that we're both on the same page and understand where this book is headed and how to follow it best, let's dive into the very first step of creating a profitable blog: determining what you will blog about and who you will be talking to.

What are you going to blog about?

This may seem counter-intuitive to you at first but bear with me.

There's this word in the "blog-o-sphere" that you may or may not be familiar with, and that's the word "niche." According to Google's dictionary, the word "niche" simply means "denoting or relating to products, services, or interests that appeal to a **small, specialized section** of the population."

And here's the counter-intuitive part: you're going to want to have as narrow a niche as you can possibly get while still having enough people interested in the topic to drive traffic.

But shouldn't it be as broad as possible so I can reach more people?

That would make sense, I know. But you're just starting out. If you try to go too broad, you'll get lost in a sea of larger, more established and trusted brands and authorities, and you'll never gain the traction you need to make a profit.

So how do you go about finding a niche that's equal parts large enough to generate traffic and small enough that you don't get lost in the sea?

Well, first you're going to just pick something

Take a few minutes to think about your hobbies, your talents, etc. What do you do for fun? What are you particularly passionate about? Do you find yourself talking about your family constantly? Or your dog? Or your garden?

I want you to do a quick test for me: for 15 minutes, brain dump as many blog post topics as you can possibly think of in as many categories as possible.

15 minutes. Go!

Once the 15 minutes are up, read back over your list. What broad categories keep popping up?

And choose one

Don't worry, you're not committed to it just yet! You can follow the process I'm going to show you with several topics if you want.

Now that you have a general idea, it's time to do some market research

There are a couple of ways to do this, and I really recommend trying it all to see what works best for you.

1. You're going to start with Google Trends. Simply type in your topic to see if it has any interest and how many people are actually searching for it.

   a. Say, for example, during your 15-minute brain dump, you thought time and time again of ideas surrounding **writing fiction**. So, you type "writing fiction" into Google Trends. Here's what you'll see:

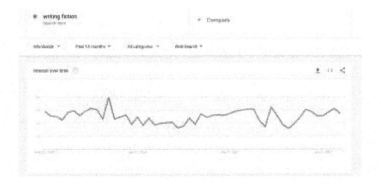

b. So, while the term "writing fiction" has certainly had its ups and downs over the past year, it's generally maintained a high level of interest.

2. Next, head over to Quora.

a. Here, you're going to type your broad term ("writing fiction") into the search bar.

b. Your search will pull up a list of the top questions people are asking about the topic. Use these questions to help you narrow down your niche even more. For example, my broad topic, "writing fiction" brings up questions about finding inspiration, getting published, the writing process, etc. Any of these things could become a niche you could potentially serve.

Determining if your niche is profitable

1. Finally, check your niche on Google AdWords Keyword Planner.

  a. Click on "Find new keywords" and type in the keywords for your niche.

  b. As you can see, our search for "writing process" shows that an average of 1,000-10,000 searches are done per month for this topic and the competition is low. Which is great!

c.   However, there's no bidding information until you get down to the keywords, "steps to writing a book." It still has 1,000-10,000 searches a month but has medium competition. While there's more competition for this search, there's also information for the bids (cost per click) businesses are making for ads in this category, which means that people are willing to pay for the services or products in this category.

All of this new wealth of information is simply to make sure that the niche you choose is a viable one for you to make money in. Hopefully, by the end of this process, you'll have a much better idea of what you will be blogging about!

Who will you be talking to?

The next step in creating a profitable blog is to get extremely clear on who your ideal customer is, what they need, and where they are headed. Being able to do this will affect every aspect of your blog and business. So while it might seem like a frivolous thing to spend your time on, understanding your ideal customer will affect what kind of content you will create, what lead magnets will work best to draw your community to you, what ad platforms you will focus on, what solutions you will provide, the words you use to describe your brand and your offer, etc. As you plan and develop your blog, you'll keep your ideal customer in mind at all times!

How to create your perfect Ideal Customer Avatar

Creating your Ideal Customer Avatar (ICA) is actually much simpler than you might expect. Just take a pen and paper (or open a Word document) and answer the following questions:

1. What goals and values does your ICA have that are relevant to the products and services you offer?

    a. Do they value family and are therefore trying to find ways to create systems in their business that'll allow them to spend more time with their family?

    b. Do they value the environment and are therefore looking for environmentally responsible products to replace products made by the major companies?

2. What books, magazines, blogs/websites, conferences, gurus, etc. would your ICA pay attention to?

    a. Where do they get their information?

3. What is their demographic information?

      a. Name, age, gender, location, marital status, number of kids, occupation, income, education, etc.

      b. Use this information to bring your ICA to life in your imagination.

4. What challenges and pain points does your ICA face that you could present a solution to?

      a. Are they mothers struggling to keep their homes clean and organized in the midst of the chaos of young kids?

      b. Are they writers who don't have a ton of money to spend, but want their books to be professional and high quality work?

5. What objections would they have to purchasing your products or services?

      a. Are they unsure they'll receive their money's worth?

      b. Do they answer to other people who ultimately decide whether or not to purchase?

Once you've followed these steps, you should have a really good idea of who your ideal customer is and what you will be blogging about. If so, you're ready to move on to the next step: building your site.

Chapter 2:

▲▼▲▼▲▼▲▼▲▼▲▼▲▼▲▼▲▼▲▼▲▼▲▼▲▼▲▼▲▼

Before you can get down to the business of blogging, you have to make sure that you have somewhere for people to find your blog. You do this by choosing a relevant and professional domain name and by setting up your website with the right host, platform, and design.

Choosing your blog's name and domain

The first thing you'll do after deciding on a niche and creating your Ideal Customer Avatar is to choose your blog's name and domain. A domain is an address for people to find your site. Because this is how people will ultimately access your content, it's important that you take time to consider what you want this name to be.

1. You could use your own name if you want to be more of a personal brand.

2. Or you could choose something that relates more to what you'll be blogging about.

If you choose the second option but have a hard time deciding on a name, you can use these steps as you consider what will be a memorable and professional name for your blog:

1. Examine other blogs in your niche to see what names they are using.

2. Think about why you're starting a blog in the first place.

    a. Of course, you're wanting to do this to make some money, but there are faster and easier ways to make money online. So, think about why you are specifically choosing to start a blog. Is it to educate people about something you're passionate about? Is it to help people find a solution to a problem they're having?

3. Consider how your readers think. What will grab their attention?

    a. This is where your Ideal Customer Avatar from Chapter 1 starts to come in!

4. Once you have a fairly extensive list, say your favorites out loud. Have other people tell you what they think.

    a. Does the one you chose make sense?

    b. Does it sound good when spoken out loud?

    c. Does it look good on the screen?

Once you've decided on the name of your blog, you'll need to decide what kind of domain you want to have. Again, there are a couple of options here:

1. If you choose to use a free site (Wordpress.com, for example), your domain name will likely look something like this:

    a. Yoursitename.wordpress.com

b. This isn't necessarily bad (and free is certainly a plus!), but it's not very professional-looking and will make it much harder for your blog to become profitable.

2. You should probably go ahead and invest in a domain name. They aren't very expensive (most costing less than $20 per year), and it will make your site look much more professional and trustworthy.

a. Yoursitename.com

b. You can also choose the extension for your domain name. For example, .com is generally the preferred domain extension, but it's becoming less and less important. It can still be pretty expensive to purchase a .com domain, though, so don't be afraid to use another, cheaper extension (like .net or .org).

c.   You can purchase your domain name on your hosting site (more on that later) or through another party. Purchasing through your hosting site is often easier and a little bit cheaper than purchasing through a third party.

Finding a host for your blog

First of all, what is a website host? A host is the provider that keeps your website files safe and makes sure people can access your site. The host is kind of like your online home—your entire site is kept and accessed from your host. Because it plays such a huge part in keeping your site secure and accessible, choosing the right host is an incredibly important decision. The good news is, though, there are several great hosting services available that are mostly pretty cheap!

What should you look for in a good blog host?

- Speed (How fast will your site load?)
- Security (How secure is your information and your content?)
- Customer support (Is customer service helpful and easy to get in touch with?)
- Additional features (What kind of additional features are available through this host?)
- Track record (What kinds of ratings and reviews do they get?)

Some services to consider:

- Bluehost
- Siteground
- HostGator
- GoDaddy

Deciding on a blogging platform

Next, you'll need to decide what content management system you'll want to use. A content management system (CMS) is where all of the writing, designing, and publishing will be done for your blog. It's where you'll spend most of your time when you're writing and publishing content for your ICA.

What should you look for in a good CMS?

- Ease of use
- Content organization
- Ability to upload images and videos
- Level of control over how your blog looks and behaves

Some services to consider

- WordPress is by far the most popular CMS available. Over 60% of all blogs run on WordPress.

o There are two options for WordPress: Wordpress.com and Wordpress.org

- **Wordpress.com** is the free version, where theme options are limited, plugins are not available, and there is very little control. Monetization of a Wordpress.com site is extremely limited.

- **Wordpress.org** is the option to choose if you are planning to make a profit from your blog (and if you're reading this book, it's likely you are). It is fully customizable, plugin options are unlimited, and you will have full control over monetization.

- Other options include:
  - o Squarespace
  - o Ghost

o   Wix

o   Blogger

Once you've chosen your blogging platform, you're ready to start designing your site! For the purposes of this book, we'll use Wordpress.org for any examples.

Choosing a theme and designing your blog

It's finally time for the fun part (at least, it's fun for me)! This is where you get to design and organize your blog with the help of a great theme. A theme is basically a template for the layout of your blog. Unless you're a web developer and can do it all on your own, choosing a good theme for your blog will make the design and organization of your site so much easier.

What should you look for in a good theme?

- Simplicity
    - You want your content to be easy to access and consume. Make sure that the theme you choose is simple, user-friendly, and gets your content in front of your readers without any kind of hassle.

- Responsiveness
    - More and more people are browsing the internet on their phones nowadays. Because of this, it's absolutely essential to make sure that your blog looks good (and is easy to use!) on both mobile devices **and** desktop/laptops.
    - You'll likely be able to tell if your site is mobile friendly from the customization page of your CMS, but

you can also run it through Google's Mobile Friendly Test page.

- Does it work in different browsers?
  - o Typically, this isn't a problem, but it's definitely good to test just in case a mistake was made in the theme's development.

- Supported plugins
  - o The ability to use plugins on your site is extremely important. On WordPress, these add-ons will give your site extra functionality for things like email list building, eCommerce support, security, etc.

- SEO optimization
  - o SEO refers to how well search engines can find your site when people search for it. Some themes aren't optimized for SEO, which makes them difficult for search engines to find.

- Customer Support

- Ratings and reviews

There are thousands of free and paid options to choose from, so take your time and choose wisely!

Once you've chosen a theme, you can get started deciding how you will serve your audience and organizing your blog to fit that purpose.

Chapter 3:

▲▼▲▼▲▼▲▼▲▼▲▼▲▼▲▼▲▼▲▼▲▼▲▼▲▼▲▼

By this point, you know who your ICA is, what they want, and where their pain points are, so you probably have an idea or two about what kinds of products or services would appeal to them.

But how do you narrow it all down to just the handful of products or services that your ICA truly needs? **Note**: For the purposes of this chapter, we'll simply say "product" when referring to products and services.

To begin, stop and think

Get a pen and paper out (or a Word document) again, and consider the following sets of questions for each product you're considering:

1. Think about exactly what this product will be:

a. What exactly will you sell? Describe the product in terms of how it will serve your ICA.

b. Briefly describe your ICA, especially if it changes a little bit from your more general ICA.

c. What price will you charge in order for it to be profitable?

d. Who will sell the product?

e. How will the product be sold?

    i. Consider sales methods and promotion processes

f. How will the product be produced?

g. How will it be paid for?

h. How will it be delivered to the customer?

i. What kind of customer service and guarantee will you provide?

2. Think about yourself:

a. A lot of the time, your ICA will be some version of yourself, whether it's you from the past (i.e. you used to have a problem but discovered a solution and are now wanting to teach other people how to solve their same problem) or you now (i.e. you currently have a problem you're learning to work through and want to bring others along on your journey). So, a good place to start when deciding what products to sell is with yourself.

b. What kinds of products do you like/find value in?

c. Do you like the product you have in mind?

d. Can you get excited about this product?

e. Would you use it yourself or recommend it to a friend or family member?

    f.   Can you see yourself promoting and selling this product for the long term?

3.   Think about it from your ICA's point of view:

    a.   How does this product help or serve your ICA?

    b.   How does this product improve your ICA's work or life?

4.   Think about it from the perspective of a management consultant:

    a.   Is there a demand for the product at the price you'll be charging?

    b.   Is the demand large enough to generate a profit?

    c.   Is your audience concentrated enough that you'll be able to advertise and deliver the product with reasonable expenses?

5.   Last few questions:

    a.   Is there a real need for the product?

    b.   How is your product better than anything else available?

    c.   What are three specific ways your product is better than your competition?

Once you've gone through these questions (ALWAYS keeping your ICA in mind), you should have a list of products or services that are designed specifically to meet your ICA's needs.

Writing product descriptions that sell

It's important to make sure that you write product descriptions that will make readers want to buy your product. This copy will tell readers what they can expect to get with the product, as well as paint a picture of what their life will be like if they choose to make the investment.

A few tips:

- Product descriptions are generally written in two sections: one in paragraph form that's heavy on description, brand voice, and emotion and another in bullet point form that lists key details about the product.

- The first paragraph should be 2-3 sentences long and focus heavily on the benefits the customer will receive if they purchase the product. It should be creative and compelling for readers, as well as giving valuable and relevant information about the product.

- The bullet points should be straightforward and to the point, listing key details about the product, such as specific things that are included, materials used to produce the product, etc.

Selling other people's products and services

We'll discuss this in more detail in chapter 8, but it is worth mentioning here that you can also make money by selling other people's products and services. This is called affiliate marketing, and it means that as you promote and sell products that have been created by other people, you receive a commission based on the purchases people make from your site. Like I said, we'll cover this more later, but keep affiliate marketing in mind as you go through this book and plan your blog.

Chapter 4:

▲▼▲▼▲▼▲▼▲▼▲▼▲▼▲▼▲▼▲▼▲▼▲▼▲▼▲▼▲▼

Once you know exactly what products and services you're going to provide, you should also consider how you're going to serve your audience for free.

I know this might be counterintuitive—the whole goal here is to make money, right? —but, the BEST way to do that is to position yourself as a generous, knowledgeable authority in your field. Offering highly valuable, free content on a weekly basis is a great way to do this. It helps to build your readers' trust in you, which will, in turn, help them in making the decision to trust you with their money. Also, if they don't need your product when they first find you, showing up consistently to serve them for free will help to keep you top-of-mind when they decide that they do need your paid products.

There are several great ways to do this with all of the technology that's available: blogging, podcasting, hosting a video show, etc. Since this book is specifically about blogging, we'll stick with that one for now.

So, you'll be producing at least one highly valuable blog post a week that will be available to your audience for free. I know that's a lot of work, but trust me, it will be worth it!

How to make a weekly publishing schedule a little less time-consuming

Basically, batching will be your best friend. Batching your blog publication means that you will write and schedule an entire month's worth of blog posts (or two months, or three, or even more if you're ambitious!) all at one time. Let's say you choose to batch two months' worth of blog posts. That means you'll prepare about eight posts within a few days. It's a lot of work during those few days, but once you're done, you can set the publication dates, and you won't have to worry about it again until it's time to prepare the next batch.

How to batch your work

1. Choose how many posts you want to finish in one batching cycle. Do you want to prepare a month in advance? Two? Three?
2. Brainstorm and choose the post topics you want to write for this batch. Come up with as many as you possibly can, then narrow them down to fit in your schedule. For this example, you'll choose eight topics (two months' worth) from your larger list.
3. Spend a day researching and outlining all of the posts for this batch.
4. Spend a couple of days writing and editing all of the posts for this batch
5. Prepare all posts for publication (create any images, materials, or freebies you want to

include; prepare your post for SEO; set a
publication date)

6. Relax until next time!

Like I said, it's a lot of work on the front end, but
you'll finish within a few days and be able to set it
aside for a few weeks.

How to write a blog post

"That's great," you might be saying, "but how do I
actually write a blog post?" Great question!

There are a few steps you should follow in writing a
blog post that will captivate your readers' attention
and leave them wanting more from you.

1. Create an outline and conduct research
    a. Your outline doesn't have to be
       incredibly detailed. It just needs to
       serve as a guide for your writing so
       that it stays organized and easy for
       readers to follow.

44

b. If you're unfamiliar with a topic, it is okay to write about it! Bloggers don't know everything, and conducting research that will yield quality information is a necessary skill to develop.

c. Take your time with this step because you want your readers to recognize you as someone who provides quality, valuable information. If your post is rambling, disorganized, or incorrect in places, readers will be less likely to trust you and your products or services.

2. Write a great headline

a. Headlines. They are the bread and butter of a blogger (or any other kind of writer, really), so learn how to write headlines that will make your readers HAVE to click through to read your post.

b. There are a few kinds of headlines you can choose from:

    i. Curiosity headlines—pique a reader's curiosity so that a reader feels compelled to read more.

    ii. How-to headlines—provide a real-life example for people to follow when they want to accomplish something.

    iii. Question headline—posing a question for your reader that the post will answer.

c. Upworthy requires its writers to come up with 25 headlines for every single piece of content, and while it might seem too difficult, you should absolutely do this too. It's hard, it's painful, it takes a long time at first, and 98% of the headlines will be horrible. BUT as you force yourself to come up with headline after headline, you'll eventually stumble upon headline gold that will make all of the effort worth it.

3. Sit down and write the post itself

   a. The best way to do this is to pound out the entire post in one sitting if at all possible. This helps to make sure that you hit all of your major points and stay on topic and organized.

4. Use images throughout your post

   a. Images break up the post and can be used for humor, to help make the post more scannable, and to illustrate complex topics or points you're needing to make.

5. Edit your post

   a. Check your post for spelling and grammar, but also the overall cohesion of the post. Does it make sense? Does one point logically follow another?

b. Check for repetition. Repetition can be a good tool for emphasis when used sparingly, but used too much, it can become jarring and even annoying for readers. Grab a thesaurus if you need to.

c. Read your post out loud. Do the sentences flow easily? Do they make sense when spoken out loud? Along the same vein, have someone else read your post, just for an added level of objectivity.

d. Understand that your post will never be perfect. Don't publish sloppy work, but don't waste hours upon hours agonizing over a single post either.

6. Hit publish!

Organizing your content

Another very important step in building a profitable blog is to make sure that your content is well-organized and easily accessible, even for the most technologically challenged of customers.

Here's a couple of tips:

- Along the top of your site, you should have a menu in a font that's easy to read and understand.
  - While it might sound fun, avoid using cutesy or clever terms for the pages of your site. Instead of saying something like "Meet the Experts," just say "About Me" or even just "About." More clever or creative terms aren't necessarily bad, but they can cause just a second of confusion for your reader, which is something we NEVER want.

Clarity and simplicity are key for developing a site that is easy to use.

- o Essential pages to have in your menu:
    - ▪ Blog
    - ▪ About
    - ▪ Services (or Products or Shop)
    - ▪ Contact
    - ▪ Any other pages that are relevant to your niche or blog
- Your content should be front-and-center everywhere your customer goes on a page. On the homepage, there should be a clear section that takes you directly to your blog posts. A sidebar on every page can guide readers to recent blog posts. You can even link to relevant blog posts inside each post.

Congratulations! Now that you've decided on a niche, created your Ideal Customer Avatar, built your site, narrowed down on how you'll serve your audience, and started producing consistent, valuable, and free content, you're ready to start welcoming people to your site!

Don't worry, though. The work's not anywhere near done!

Chapter 5:

If you thought the hard work was done, think again! If you've narrowed down on your niche and your ideal customer, built a professional and user-friendly website, decided what specific products and services you will provide for your customers, and started showing up weekly for your audience with free, valuable content, it's finally time to learn how to get eyes on your content and products!

It's kind of crazy how many social media platforms are available, though! If you're not careful, you could easily spend all of your time trying to figure them all out and spread yourself too thin. When you're just starting out, though, it's actually better to focus in on one or two (MAYBE three) platforms instead of trying to tackle them all at once. But how do you decide which are the best ones to start with?

Here are a few ways to narrow it down:

1. Identify your social media goals
   a. Everything you do in your blog/business should have a clear purpose, and that's especially true when making decisions like this. Once you have a clear purpose for your social media marketing, you can consider the benefits and purposes of each platform to decide which are most aligned with your own purpose.
   b. Do you want to use social media to provide great customer service and interact with people? If so, Facebook or Twitter might be good options because they both involve high customer interaction and a strong messaging interface.
   c. Do you want to exhibit products or services? LinkedIn might be your

platform of choice because of the
number of people there who are
actively searching for services or
products.

2. Make sure you have a deep understanding of
who your ICA is.

   a. Do some research to see where your
   ICA's demographic hangs out the
   most. If your ICA is a female between
   the ages of 25 and 35 whose
   household income is about
   $80,000/year and who is interested in
   home organization, cooking, and
   raising her children, Pinterest might be
   a great place to start!

   b. What kind of business are you? If you
   are business to business (B2B),
   LinkedIn might be a great place to
   generate leads, since 46% of traffic to
   B2B websites comes from LinkedIn.
   On the other hand, if you are business

to consumer (B2C), you should be more interested in sites like Facebook and Twitter that provide much more opportunity for customer interaction.

c. **Note**: Business to Business simply means that you sell products and services to businesses, while Business to Consumer means that you sell products and services directly to consumers.

3. Finally, you should have an idea of the kind of content you want to post.

a. If you are interested in creating short, simple videos, Snapchat or Instagram would be great. If you're interested in giving short, to-the-point updates or posts, check out Twitter. If you want to create beautiful visual content that will lead directly to your site, Pinterest is the way to go. If you want kind of a catch-all platform that allows pretty much any kind of content, Facebook and Google+ are where you should start.

Next steps

Now that you've chosen a couple of platforms to focus on first, here's how you can make sure that you're taking advantage of everything your platforms have to offer.

1. Spend some quality time with your profile. Take the time to write a company or personal bio, a mission statement, your availability (if applicable), and any other relevant information. The most important thing about your profile will be a link that will take viewers directly to your site. Your profile will be a kind of introduction to who you are as a person and as a company and will give viewers an idea of what they can expect from you. So, make sure that your profile is

professional, polished, and optimized to get people interested in who you are.

2. Once your profile is set up on each of your platforms, start promoting your content! Every time you publish a new blog post (so, every week, at least), announce it by giving a short, intriguing quote from the post and providing a link that will take readers directly to the post. You can also repurpose older content by quoting different portions of the article, asking your audience relevant questions about the article, and publishing a variety of images related to the article. Every few months, you should change the headline and update any information that might have become irrelevant or inaccurate. Also, make sure that you promote other people's valuable content! Like so many things in this book so far, this might seem counterintuitive at first, but by curating valuable content (besides just your own) for your readers, you are staying

top-of-mind for them and positioning yourself as a generous source of information. You're letting your readers know that you care about them and that they get the results they need, regardless of where those results come from. A generally accepted rule of thumb for this practice is that 80% of your content should be curated content from other people, while 20% should be promoting your own content.

3. Give your readers an EASY way to share your posts.

   a. Much of the time, people measure the influence of a website by how many shares it earns. A site with a lot of shares on social media is likely to be more easily trusted than one that has only been shared a few times. To encourage readers to share your post, you need to make it extremely easy for them to do so. You can do this by

embedding a social media sharing tool
on each post and page on your site
and by including a Click to Tweet
quote within your posts.

4. Post when your audience is active

a. Do some research to discover when
your ideal customer is likely to be
active on social media. Hubspot has a
great article that will give you a lot of
great information about when to post
on various social media platforms.

5. Focus on visual content

a. Content with a visual component is 40
times more likely to be shared on
social media, so make sure to use
intriguing, quality photos, graphs, info
graphs, videos, or animations to
capture your audience's attention.

b. Canva is great place to design these
graphics! It is completely free to use
(of course, they do offer paid plans

that provide even more great tools)
and is incredibly user-friendly.

6. Engage consistently

   a. Participate in discussions and chats,
   respond when people engage with
   you, and start conversations on your
   own. As your brand and your platform
   grow, people will love getting to hear
   directly from you. It helps to create a
   sense of camaraderie and trust
   between yourself and your audience.

7. Use a clear call-to-action within each post!

   a. Tell the reader exactly what you want
   them to do with the post you've
   shown them.

   b. Test your CTAs—write down a list of
   several you could use. Use each one at
   least 5 times and keep track of the
   metrics (how often people follow the
   CTA).

      i. Click Here

      ii.   Read/Learn More

      iii. Visit Our Site

8. Try paid advertising

    a. If you're just starting out, it might be difficult to invest in paid advertising on social media. However, if you can set aside at least a small budget for it, you'll be able to reach many more people who haven't yet heard of you or your brand.

    b. When you create an ad, make sure to promote a link to a blog post (and a highly-valuable freebie—more on that later!) as opposed to a product. If someone has never heard of you before, they aren't likely to click through to view a product they'll have to pay for. It's much more likely that they'll be interested in what you have to say about the given topic and in the freebie you provide. Later, once they've become more used to you and trust you a little bit more, you can refer them to various products or services you sell.

Succeeding on social media might take some trial and error, but if you keep at it, you'll be able to drive the traffic you need to your blog so that you can start developing your very own loyal fan base.

Chapter 6:

▲▼▲▼▲▼▲▼▲▼▲▼▲▼▲▼▲▼▲▼▲▼▲▼▲▼▲▼▲▼

Thus far in this book, we've covered quite a bit: niche, ideal customer avatars, building a website, products, and services, writing and organizing blog posts, and gaining traffic with social media. By now, you should be in the very early stages of your blogging business. You've probably spent some time designing your site, you might have a few posts up, and perhaps you've even gotten a few shares on your social media platforms. Now how do you go about converting your trickle of relatively unengaged traffic into loyal customers?

Email Lists

Yep, we're taking a step back in time to talk about a type of technology that's much older than beautiful, user-friendly websites and social media platforms. It might seem strange (so much in this book probably does), but email lists really are where it's at when it comes to nurturing loyal customers.

What makes email lists so important to your business?

- You have complete control over your email list. Unlike social media platforms, which you don't own, your email list is yours. Social media platforms can (and have) changed overnight (seemingly to those of us who use them for marketing). Facebook recently changed their entire algorithm, obliging us to pay in order for people to see our posts. It's truly unfortunate. But what are you going to do? Facebook owns Facebook, so it can pretty much do what it wants. Your email list, though, is completely your own! Your newsletters can include any information you want it to include. They can go out to as many people on your list as you want. It's all yours.

- People who click through to subscribe are much more likely to buy your products or services. They're people who take action, and they've taken an action to invite you into their personal email inbox. That's basically like being invited into a person's online home. People are much pickier about who they allow into their inbox than who they follow on social media, so take full advantage of their interest and engagement! Ask them questions, talk with them, and engage with them. It's incredible, but once you start actually selling your products or services, the people on your email list will be the ones who are most enthusiastic.

- It's easy to keep in touch with your audience via email. Big announcements can easily be shared in a weekly/bi-weekly/monthly newsletter addressed **directly** to your fans. Almost everyone checks their email at least once a day, even if they go a few days without

checking social media, and there your name
will be, along with new and valuable content,
personal engagement, and other strategies that
will help nurture your list into loyal
customers.

To make all of this information a little more clear,
Direct Marketing Association has found that email
marketing has shown an average of 4,300% return on
investment for businesses in the U.S. That's pretty
darn incredible, and if you don't take advantage, you'll
definitely be missing out.

How to build an email list

Now that you're convinced that you need an email list
(you are convinced, right?), let's talk about some
practical stuff.

1. Choose an email marketing service. There are
    a ton of great ones available, and you'll need
    to decide which one is best for your business
    and your budget.

    a. Mailchimp, Convertkit, and AWeber are some great ones to start with.

    b. On these sites, you can set up your list and list segments, as well as the campaigns you'll be sending out to them.

2. Make sure that you're creating consistent, valuable content for your audience. This is probably the most foundational step in building an engaged email list, so make sure you don't neglect your blog in favor of social media, your email list, or even your products or services.

3. Give people an incentive to sign up! This is often called a freebie, an opt-in incentive, or a lead magnet. You can offer a free eBook, free templates, a checklist, a cheat sheet, a guide, etc. OptinMonster provides a really great article on some of the most effective lead magnets. The idea is that people will trade

their email address in order to receive the valuable freebie you are offering.

    a. When deciding what kind of lead-magnet you want to create, there are a few things to consider:

        i. Does your lead magnet solve a specific problem for your ICA?

        ii. Does your lead magnet promise a quick win for your ICA?

        iii. This doesn't mean that all of their problems are solved! That will only come through one of your paid offers. But your lead magnet should prove to your audience that you can deliver the solutions they need.

    b. Can you deliver your lead magnet immediately?

c. Is your lead magnet super specific?

d. Does your lead magnet offer something that's high value for your ICA?

e. Is your lead magnet quick and easy to understand and use?

f. Does your lead magnet demonstrate that you know your stuff and can lead them to achieve their goals?

4. Give your audience MULTIPLE opportunities to sign up for your email list. Include an opt-in incentive at the end of every blog post, as well as in a sidebar form, a popup, and/or an in-line form. You can also change up your freebie. One way to do this is by creating a "content upgrade," which is simply an opt-in incentive/freebie that relates to a particular blog post. For example, if you're writing a blog post about the best lead magnets to create for a blog, you might include an easy-to-digest list of lead magnets

that's organized by effectiveness. Include a sign-up form for your content upgrade within the post and at the end of the post. Have a popup form appear as a reader gets through about half of the page or as they're about to leave the page. Then, in the sidebar, continue to include a sign-up form for your main freebie/incentive. It might feel like a bit much to you, but your reader will likely only notice one or two of these sign-up opportunities, so you need to make sure there are plenty of them available.

5. Enlist your list to share your content for you by including a share feature within each email. Doing this will get your content in front of even more people you would never have access to on your own.

6. Test a variety of calls-to-action. Like we discussed in the last chapter, though, you need to always make sure that your CTA is extremely clear for your audience. Don't give

them a chance to guess what you want them to do. Tell them to do something specific, like "Sign Up Now!"

7. Keep on keeping on. This process can be a slow one, especially at first. Generating traffic that leads to engaged and loyal fans will take some time, but if you keep at it, you'll find that it will be well worth the effort.

One last note

It's important that you start building your email list as early as possible, even if you only have a couple of posts up, a nearly invisible trickle of traffic, and your site isn't even fully developed yet. Starting early will help you develop the habits and strategies you'll need in order to compound your email list growth. And, in the meantime, you won't miss out on opportunities for people to engage with you. Those few people who pop by in the early days of your business are just as viable leads as ones who jump on board later. In fact, they might end up being your most loyal fans, since they got the opportunity to grow with you and watch your blog and business develop over time.

In the next chapter, we'll talk about how to use your growing email list to start generating a profit! Now we're getting to the good stuff!

Chapter 7:

▲▼▲▼▲▼▲▼▲▼▲▼▲▼▲▼▲▼▲▼▲▼▲▼▲▼▲▼▲▼

Now that you know a little bit about how to grow your email list, it's time to put that list to use! Like we discussed, your email list is a gold mine for revenue because the people who opt-in to your email are more active, engaged, and enthusiastic than any follower on social media will be. Though if they're a follower on social media AND subscribe to your email list, you just might have a super fan on your hands! Hooray! But how do you make money with your email list in a way that's effective and service-oriented?

Here are some tips and tricks for making money with your email list:

- Sell a product or service via a tripwire IMMEDIATELY upon sign-up.
    - o A tripwire is simply a next-step offer that's given immediately after a person signs up for your email list. It's

extremely affordable, making it easy for them to decide to purchase (usually in the $5-$20 range). It often relates to the freebie they signed up for and acts as a next step to purchasing your higher-priced products or services.

  o When someone signs up for your email list, immediately send them to a tripwire landing page where they can read about your offer and make the decision to purchase. It's at this point that the customer is most excited about you and your brand, so take advantage of their excitement to offer them something of high value for an extremely affordable price.

- Stay top-of-mind for your email subscribers by showing up in their inbox regularly.

  o When someone signs up for your email list, make sure to have a welcome email in their inbox within minutes. This welcome email should deliver the freebie you promised, as well as introduce yourself and your business and give the subscriber an idea of what they can expect from you in the future.

o Start writing a regular newsletter, whether it's weekly, bi-weekly, or monthly. A newsletter is a great way to show up in your subscribers' inbox regularly without being too sales-y. You can inform your list about new posts you've published, provide additional, exclusive content, and ask them to engage with you in various ways.

- Remind subscribers of your services or products in each email—but do it subtly.

  o The majority of your emails should provide free and valuable content to your subscribers (remember the 80/20 rule). However, even inside the newsletters you send out regularly, a subtle reminder of your products is definitely appropriate (and smart!).

- Segment your list
  - o Having one large email list is great, for sure. But you should also divide your list into segments to send even more targeted offers. You can segment your list by demographics, interests, open rates, past purchases, etc. to help make sure that the most relevant information is being sent out to your subscribers.

- Catch abandoned carts before it's too late
  - o When someone clicks through to purchase something but ultimately abandons their cart, you should have an autoresponder ready to go to catch those potential clients and find out

why they chose not to buy. Once you know why they chose not to buy, you can try to allay their specific concerns, so they return to their cart and finish the purchase.

- Promote your offer
  - o Every once in a while (not too often, though!), you can send a special promotion out to your email list. Offer a limited-time discount for a premium product or provide additional bonuses that give even more value to the customer. This kind of direct promotion will give you a burst of revenue, while also reminding people of the offers you have, so if they choose not to buy during the promotion, they might come back to it later.
- Up-sell

o   When someone makes a purchase
from you, offer an upgrade or another
product that relates to the one they
initially purchased. This upgrade
should, as always, provide even more
value to the customer and can even
complement their first purchase in a
way that both are more effective when
purchased together.

Now that we've covered the most foundational and
long-term ways of building a profitable blog, in the
next chapter, we'll go over some other ways you can
make a consistent living from your blog.

Chapter 8:

▲▼▲▼▲▼▲▼▲▼▲▼▲▼▲▼▲▼▲▼▲▼▲▼▲▼▲▼▲▼

Thus far in this book, we've talked a lot about the process of building a blog that's designed to generate a profit, and we've touched a little on some practical ways to make that happen (namely through selling products or services and promoting them via email marketing). But there are actually so many other ways to make money as a blogger, and in this chapter, we'll dive deeper into some of them.

How much money can a blogger make

Although it's impossible to give a specific amount you can make as a blogger, I can tell you that there's pretty much no limit on how much you can make. Of course, only a few bloggers are lucky enough to make millions of dollars every year. In fact, the vast majority make very little money at all. But, with some skill, some creativity, and a LOT of hard work and perseverance, it is absolutely possible to make a healthy full-time living.

How to make money as a blogger

Advertising

- Much like magazines and newspapers sell ads, bloggers can sell real estate on their websites to advertisers. Many bloggers start off with an ad network like Google AdSense since dealing directly with an advertiser requires a certain level of traffic. However, advertising is a great way to start making money with your blog.

- Here are several ways you can make money through advertising. Spend some time researching some of them to see if they could be profitable for you:
    - o Ad networks
    - o Brand ambassadorships
    - o Sponsored posts
    - o Sponsored social content

- ○ Job boards
- ○ Newsletter advertising
- ○ Video advertising
- ○ Podcast advertising
- ○ Competitions and giveaways

Affiliate Programs

- Affiliate income is when you provide a link to a product that's sold on another site. If someone follows your link and buys the product, you earn a certain percentage of the profit from that sale. Affiliate programs are another great way to start because they're easy to sign up for and, while it helps to have a good amount of traffic visiting your blog, it only takes one person to click through your link to start earning commission on your affiliate product.

- There are literally thousands of affiliate programs you can join, but here's a short list to get you started:

- o Amazon Associates
- o <u>Amazon Influencer Program</u>
- o Bluehost (or another hosting service—preferably the one you choose to use for your own blog)
- o Ultimate Bundles
- o Genesis—premium WordPress themes

Hosting Events

- This can be anything from a huge conference (probably not something you should try right out of the gate) to small get-togethers for you and your audience. In either case, you make money by charging for attendance and/or by finding a company to sponsor the event.
- These can also be online events or summits, which are much cheaper and easier to implement.

Recurring Income

- Lots of bloggers are starting to charge a recurring (monthly/annual) fee for access to a premium community, exclusive content, tools, and/or coaching. These are basically memberships that readers pay to participate in or have access to.

Promoting a Physical Business

- Blogs can be used to drive customers to a physical store or business. The point of this kind of blog is not so much to make money on its own but to grow their online presence and point their audience to the physical store where the money will be made.

Providing Services or Products

- We've been talking about this throughout the book, but it's worth mentioning again here. If you have a particular skill, a solution to a particular problem, or a product you can sell, by all means, use your blog to sell it! Services can be anything from coaching, to writing, to graphic or web design, to any other freelance service. Products could be either virtual or physical and can range from eBooks, to courses, to t-shirts, to workbooks.

- Examples of products or services you can provide:
  - Coaching
  - Training
  - Consulting
  - Speaking
  - Graphic design
  - Web design
  - Copywriting
  - eBooks
  - Courses
  - Software
  - Printables
  - Apps
  - Books
  - Workbooks

  o Merchandise

Other Steams of Income

- Donations
- Selling your blog
- Syndication

Prepare to have multiple streams of income

The best way to make a consistent living as a blogger is to make sure that you have multiple streams of income. It means you won't have all of your eggs in one basket, and if one income stream performs very poorly one month, it's likely that another will pick up the slack somehow.

Prepare to constantly produce valuable, free content

This is how you position yourself as a trustworthy, knowledgeable source of information, and it's precisely how your blog will have success for the long-term. Without making this a core foundation of your blogging career, you might have some fleeting success, but it will be difficult to sustain.

Find one or two bloggers to model and learn from, but DON'T try to copy them!

Be yourself! It's definitely wise to find a couple of bloggers to model yourself after, but you should never try to imitate them exactly. Part of what will make your blog and brand attractive is your unique personality and spin on what you do as a blogger. Another word of caution: I said to find a couple of bloggers to model, emphasis on "a **couple**." Don't get caught up with following dozens of bloggers. It will only take up a lot of the time and energy that you should be spending on your blog.

Chapter 9:

▲▼▲▼▲▼▲▼▲▼▲▼▲▼▲▼▲▼▲▼▲▼▲▼▲▼▲▼▲▼

Now that you have a great foundation for starting your own profitable blog, it's time to get started! With any profession, though, there are tons and tons of tools available that can help you. There's so many; it can be overwhelming. So, in this chapter, I've compiled a list of some of the tools I've used or researched that can give you a good place to start as you try to make these decisions for yourself. By all means, do your own research and decide based on what you think is best for your blog. This is by no means a comprehensive list, and there are many other tools out there that you can use as well.

Hosting

- Bluehost
    - o Bluehost is one of the best hosting sites available. It's affordable, scalable, offers 1-click WordPress installation (a

great feature, by the way!), as well as a free SSL certificate to make sure that you and your visitors are protected. It also offers great 24/7 support.

- Siteground
  - o Siteground is another really great host. They also have great support, 1-click WordPress installation (really, it's a must for a host to offer!), a 30-day money back guarantee, and are both affordable and scalable. Do your research to decide what host is best for you. Check out each website and look at their ratings and reviews.

Email service providers

- Mailchimp
  - o Mailchimp is a great email marketing service to start out with because it's

actually completely free until your list grows to 1,000 subscribers! Hopefully, that won't take very long, but by the time you have 1,000 subscribers, it's likely you'll be making enough from your blog to be able to invest in one of their paid plans or another email service. Mailchimp offers the ability to send targeted emails and newsletters to your list, build landing pages for your products and services, design ads, and lots more.

- Convertkit
    - Convertkit is among the most used and most loved email providers out there. It does come with a bit of investment (their lowest package is $29/month), but it was designed with creative entrepreneurs in mind (another way of saying technologically challenged/disinterested). It's very

easy and intuitive to use, and it offers even more advanced segmentation and automation abilities.

Learning about blogging/marketing

- Problogger
    - Problogger offers a vast amount of valuable, FREE content around how to start, grow, and sustain a profitable blog. The owner, Darren Rowse also hosts a podcast that provides even more valuable information, as well as encouraging and motivating case studies of everyday people who have succeeded in the blogging world. Along with all of this free content, Problogger offers paid eCourses, eBooks, and other training materials that can help you get your blogging business up and running successfully.
- Amy Porterfield

o Amy Porterfield is a fantastic resource for learning how to use online marketing strategies. She hosts a well-known podcast called *The Online Marketing Made Easy Podcast*, where she provides extremely actionable and practical advice for growing your business online. She also offers great courses on building an email list and creating online courses.

Monetization

- Teachable
  - o Teachable is a course hosting platform that offers everything you will need to sell and deliver professional and valuable courses.
- PayPal and Stripe
  - o Both options provide a secure and well-established payment system.

- Zoom
  - o Zoom is extremely useful for meeting with your clients 1-on-1 or hosting live webinars.

- Gumroad
  - o You can use this platform to sell and deliver digital products like planners, workbooks, etc.

Landing Pages

- LeadPages
  - o This site is pretty much amazing. It is extremely easy to use and helpful (It actually tells you how well your landing page is likely to convert and what you can do to improve it.) You can use it to create landing pages, sales pages, thank you pages, popups, banners, and lots more.

- OptinMonster

- o Similar service to LeadPages—just another option for you! Do your research to decide which one is best for your business.

SEO

- Google Keyword Planner
  - o Use Google's own suggestions for which keywords you should use in your blog posts. Better yet, it's free!
- Long Tail Pro
  - o Long Tail Pro is not free. BUT it is extremely powerful for finding long-tail keywords.
- Ubersuggest
  - o Yet another tool to find suggestions as to what keywords you should use.
- Yoast
  - o Hands-down the best SEO plugin out there. It will analyze your blog post

inside the WordPress editor and give you specific steps you can take to improve your readability score and your SEO score.

Productivity

- Trello
  - An incredibly flexible and useful tool for managing your tasks, workflows, and other productivity and organizational needs.
- Self Control App (Mac only)
  - A free application that allows you to temporarily block access to certain websites (I'm looking at you, Facebook, you time-sucking vortex!).
- Google Drive
  - Reliable cloud storage for all of your blog files, images, etc. It's also great for working with a team since you can

share access with other people who can then edit and add to the drive.

- Mindmeister
  - An excellent mind-mapping tool that will help you brainstorm and organize your thoughts.

Design/Branding

- Canva
  - Canva is a great and easy-to-use platform for creating high-quality graphics. And, best of all, it's free to use (though it does offer a paid option).
- Adobe
  - This is certainly a pricy option, and it will take a while to learn how to use all of the tools that are available. But if you can stomach the cost and the time it takes to learn how to use it, Adobe

offers the best software available for creating stunning graphics, PDFs, logos, etc. There's definitely a reason it's so pricey.

- Unsplash and Pexels
  - o Both of these sites offer beautiful stock photos for free.
- Coolors.co
  - o This site is pretty useful for creating color schemes that work well together, whether you're deciding on your brand colors, a color scheme for a PDF workbook, or you just need ideas for how to paint your house.

Analytics

- Google Analytics
  - o Google Analytics is the most robust analytics application for website owners. It's completely free and

provides comprehensive details on your website visitors.

Marketing/Social Media

- Tailwind
    - Tailwind allows you to schedule posts on Pinterest and Instagram. It also provides great analytics and insights into what works and what doesn't. It makes marketing on Pinterest and Instagram so much faster and organized!
- Buffer
    - Another great social media scheduling tool. Do some research on both to decide what will work best for your blog and business.

Writing

- Grammarly

o   Grammarly is great for simple
    proofreading. It helps you find and
    correct errors and even suggests better
    words you can use to clarify your
    writing.

- Coschedule's Headline Analyzer

    o   This tool is amazing for analyzing
        your headlines and giving you tips for
        making them even better.

Conclusion

▲▼▲▼▲▼▲▼▲▼▲▼▲▼▲▼▲▼▲▼▲▼▲▼▲▼▲▼▲▼▲▼▲▼

Thank you for making it through to the end of *Blogging for Profit: The No-Nonsense Beginner's Blueprint to Earn Money Online with Your Blog.* Let's hope it was informative and able to provide you with all of the tools you need to achieve your goals, whatever they may be.

The next step is to get started building your own blog! Purchasing and reading this book was a great start toward that goal, but now it's up to you to take what you learned here and use it. Throughout this book, I tried to provide a step-by-step process that's easy to follow, so you can use this book as a guide for growing your own profitable blog.

Phil C. Senior

Connect with us on our Facebook page

www.facebook.com/bluesourceandfriends and stay

tuned to our latest book promotions and free

giveaways.